W9-CHE-428

from SEA TO SHINING SEA

VERMONT

By Dennis Brindell Fradin

CONSULTANTS

Roy Zirblis, M.S., Consultant, Historical Research;
Past Editor, *The Green Mountaineer*

Paul Donovan, M.L.S., Senior Reference Librarian, Vermont Department of Libraries

Robert L. Hillerich, Ph.D., Consultant, Pinellas County Schools, Florida;
Visiting Professor, University of South Florida

CHILDRENS PRESS®
CHICAGO

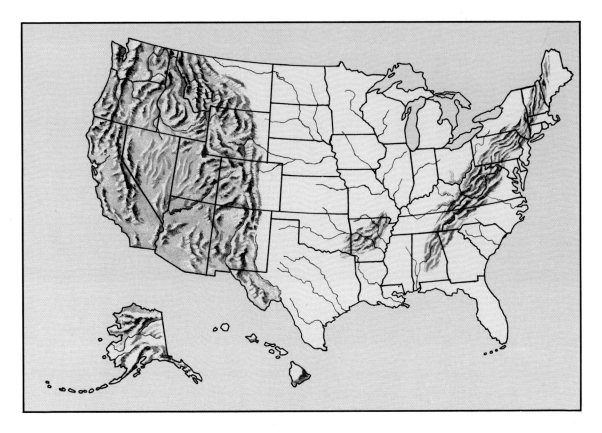

Vermont is one of the six states in the region called New England. The other New England states are Connecticut, Maine, Massachusetts, New Hampshire, and Rhode Island.

For my sister, Lori Fradin

Front cover picture: a covered bridge in Grafton; page 1, the village of Waits River; back cover, winter on the Middlebury River near Ripton

Project Editor: Joan Downing
Design Director: Karen Kohn
Research Assistant: Judith Bloom Fradin
Typesetting: Graphic Connections, Inc.
Engraving: Liberty Photoengraving

Library of Congress Cataloging-in-Publication Data

Fradin, Dennis B.
  Vermont / by Dennis Brindell Fradin.
    p. cm. — (From sea to shining sea)
  Includes index.
  Summary: An introduction to the history, geography, important people, and interesting sites of Vermont.
  ISBN 0-516-03845-1
  1. Vermont—Juvenile literature. I. Title. II. Series: Fradin, Dennis B. From sea to shining sea.
F49.3.F68 1993   92-36371
974.3—dc20   CIP
                                        AC

Table of Contents

The St. Johnsbury band is the third-oldest band in the country.

Introducing the Green Mountain State

The settlers named them the Green Mountains because of the green trees on their slopes.

Vermont is a state in the northeastern United States. Its nickname is the "Green Mountain State." The Green Mountains run down the middle of Vermont. The name *Vermont* comes from the French words *vert mont*. They mean "green mountain."

Ethan Allen and his Green Mountain Boys are Vermont's most famous heroes. They fought for the Americans in the Revolutionary War. During that war, Vermont declared itself an independent country. In 1791, Vermont became part of the United States.

Today, Vermont is a popular vacationland. In the spring, visitors enjoy watching maple syrup being made. Vermont leads the country at producing this. Vermont's cool summers bring many people to the state. Each fall, "leaf peepers" visit Vermont to see its colorful trees. In winter, people go there to ski.

The Green Mountain State is special in other ways. Which state first outlawed slavery? Where was the country's first teacher-training school? Where was America's first Boy Scout troop founded?

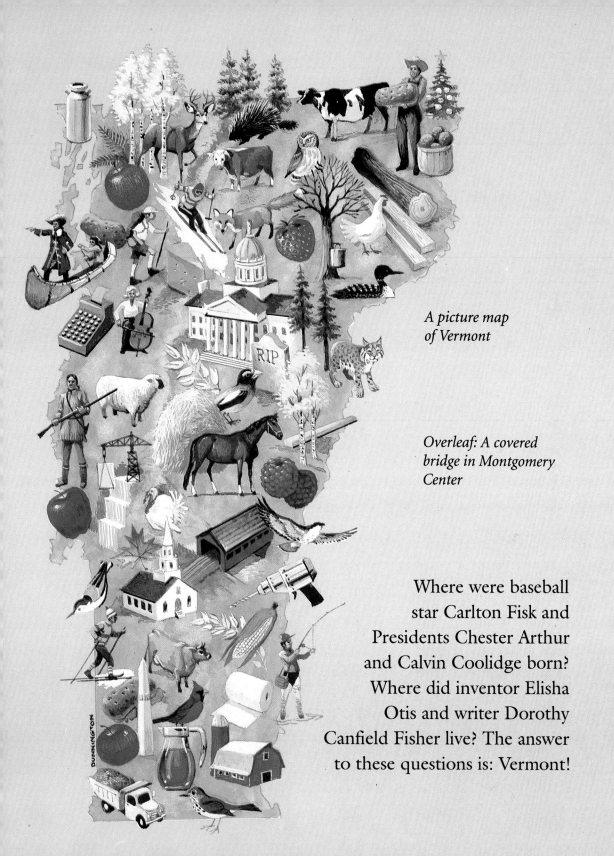

A picture map of Vermont

Overleaf: A covered bridge in Montgomery Center

Where were baseball star Carlton Fisk and Presidents Chester Arthur and Calvin Coolidge born? Where did inventor Elisha Otis and writer Dorothy Canfield Fisher live? The answer to these questions is: Vermont!

5

A Land of Mountains, Woods, and Waters

A Land of Mountains, Woods, and Waters

Vermont is one of the New England states. The other five New England states are Maine, New Hampshire, Massachusetts, Rhode Island, and Connecticut. Of the New England states, only Maine is larger than Vermont. But of all fifty states, Vermont is the eighth smallest. It covers only 9,614 square miles.

The Connecticut River forms Vermont's eastern border with New Hampshire. Lake Champlain forms most of Vermont's western border with New York. Massachusetts is to the south. Another country—Canada—is north of Vermont.

Bottom right: The Connecticut River, near Newbury

TOPOGRAPHY

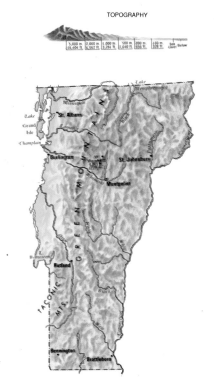

As its nickname shows, Vermont is mountain-ous. The Green Mountains are in the middle of the state. The state's highest peak, Mount Mansfield, is there. Mount Mansfield stands 4,393 feet above sea level. The Taconic Mountains are in southwest Vermont. The White Mountains are in the northeast part of the state.

Three-fourths of Vermont is forest. The sugar maple is the state tree. Poplars, birches, spruces, hemlocks, and pines are other common trees.

Above: Three-fourths of Vermont is forest. Below: Mt. Mansfield

Lake Champlain

The Connecticut River is controlled by New Hampshire.

About 430 lakes and ponds add splashes of blue to Vermont's map. Vermont has one very large lake. This is Lake Champlain. It covers about 440 square miles. About two-thirds of Lake Champlain is in northwestern Vermont. The rest is in New York and Canada. Vermont's longest river is Otter Creek. It flows into Lake Champlain.

Vermont's woods and waters are home to many kinds of animals. Deer, foxes, and bears live in Vermont. Beavers, porcupines, bobcats, and moose are also found in the state.

10

CLIMATE

Vermont's winters are long and cold. Temperatures often drop below minus 10 degrees Fahrenheit. Vermont's record low was minus 50 degrees Fahrenheit. This was recorded at Bloomfield on December 30, 1933. Few states have ever measured a colder temperature. Skiers love the 100 inches of snow that fall on Vermont's mountains each year.

Vermont's record high temperature was 105 degrees Fahrenheit. It was recorded at Vernon on July 4, 1911. But Vermont's summers tend to be short and cool. Snow usually falls before the end of October. "Summer is short around here. Last year, it was on a Thursday," is an old Vermont saying.

In Vermont, it is common for snow to fall even before the trees have lost their autumn leaves.

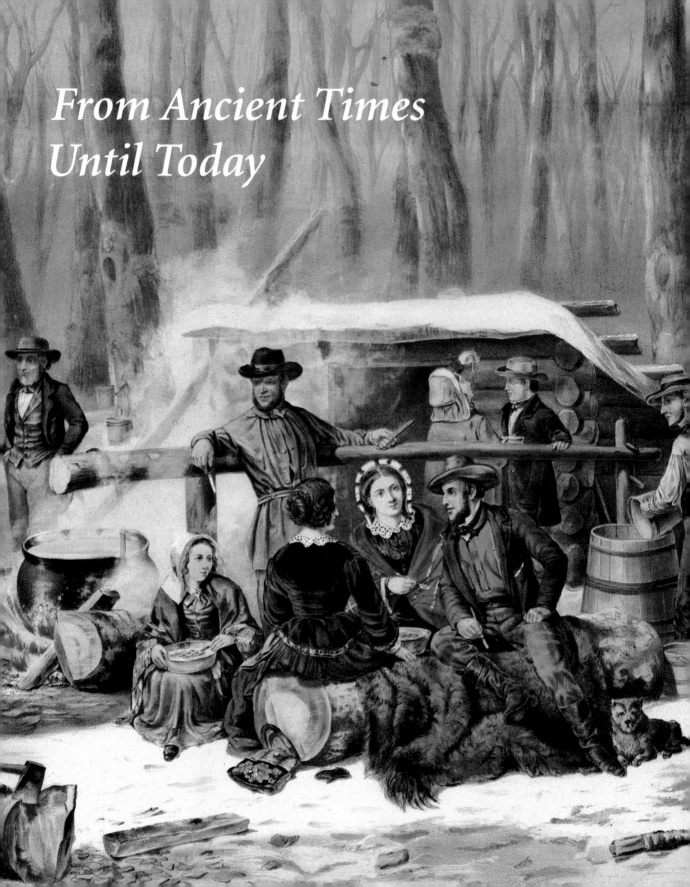

*From Ancient Times
Until Today*

FROM ANCIENT TIMES UNTIL TODAY

The Green Mountains are old, even for mountains. They were forced up out of the earth about 450 million years ago. When they were young, the Green Mountains were very tall. Over millions of years, however, water wore away at their peaks.

The Ice Age began about two million years ago. Huge ice sheets called glaciers spread out from the north. All of Vermont was under ice. The glaciers scattered rocks across Vermont. They also dug holes. Those holes later filled with water. They became lakes and ponds.

VERMONT'S EARLY PEOPLE

Ancient Indians reached Vermont about 12,000 years ago. Their spear points and pottery have been found. Much later, several American Indian groups lived in the region. They included the Abenakis and Mahicans. Those groups used Vermont as a hunting ground. They hunted bears and deer with bows and arrows. They also grew corn, beans, and squash. They traveled along the streams by canoe. For

Opposite: A detail from a Currier lithograph of a maple sugar party near a sugar house

Long, long ago, glaciers dug holes in Vermont that later filled with water and became lakes.

13

Early American Indians carved these pictures on the rocks along the Connecticut River near Bellows Falls.

winter travel, the Indians made snowshoes. Vermont's Indians learned to make maple syrup by boiling sap from maple trees.

The Indians had no written language before Europeans arrived. Yet, they had a kind of picture writing. Examples can be seen carved in rocks at Bellows Falls.

FRENCH AND ENGLISH CLAIMS IN VERMONT

France began settling Canada in 1604. French explorers soon went south, toward Vermont. In 1609, French explorer Samuel de Champlain became the first known European to reach Vermont. He explored Lake Champlain. He named it for himself. Champlain claimed Vermont for France. In 1666, the French built Fort St. Anne on Isle La Motte. The island is in Lake Champlain.

By that time, England had settled most of its thirteen colonies. They were along the Atlantic Ocean. In 1690, English soldiers from New York entered Vermont. They built a fort near what is now Addison.

Between 1689 and 1763, England and France fought for control of North America. Many Indians helped the French. England's Massachusetts colony feared an attack by Indians coming down through Vermont. They wanted protection. So, in 1724, Massachusetts settlers built Fort Dummer in southeastern Vermont. Fort Dummer was near present-day Brattleboro. The fort was Vermont's first permanent non-Indian settlement.

England finally defeated France in 1763. This meant that England would rule Vermont.

THE NEW HAMPSHIRE GRANTS

Even before 1763, Vermont was not a separate English colony. Instead, land there was claimed by two of England's colonies. Both the New Hampshire and New York colonies believed they owned Vermont land.

Benning Wentworth became New Hampshire's governor in 1741. Governor Wentworth granted Vermont land to relatives, to friends, and even to himself. Between 1749 and 1763, Wentworth granted half the land that later became Vermont. The region was not yet called Vermont, though. It was called the New Hampshire Grants.

New York claimed Vermont, too. New York's governor granted parts of Vermont to New Yorkers. In 1764, the king of England ruled that Vermont

Benning Wentworth

Ethan Allen and the Green Mountain Boys fought against the New Yorkers who tried to settle on land in the New Hampshire Grants.

"Catamount" is short for "cat of the mountains."

belonged to New York. Colonists with New Hampshire Grants would have to pay New York for their land. Otherwise, they might lose it.

THE GREEN MOUNTAIN BOYS

The settlers on the Grants had already paid New Hampshire. Many of them refused to pay New York as well. In 1770, a group of Vermonters joined together to fight New York's claim. They called themselves the Green Mountain Boys. Ethan Allen was their leader. Seth Warner was an important member.

The Green Mountain Boys met at a Bennington tavern. They placed a stuffed catamount (mountain lion) outside the tavern. The catamount was a warning from the Green Mountain Boys. They would pounce like catamounts on New Yorkers who tried to get their land. The meeting place became known as the Catamount Tavern.

The Green Mountain Boys sometimes whipped New Yorkers. They also stole their cattle. Such treatment drove many New Yorkers out of Vermont. By 1775, the fight over Vermont was not yet settled. Something happened, however, that pushed the argument aside.

The Revolutionary War

In April 1775, the thirteen colonies began fighting to free themselves from England. This is called the Revolutionary War (1775-1783). Vermont was not one of the colonies. It was still claimed by both New Hampshire and New York. But many Vermonters helped the colonies win the war.

Ethan Allen decided to capture Fort Ticonderoga, in New York. On May 10, 1775, Allen took the fort by surprise. Not a shot was fired. Two days later, Seth Warner captured the English fort at Crown Point, New York.

The Battle of Hubbardton was the only Revolutionary War battle fought in Vermont. The

Ethan Allen and his men captured Fort Ticonderoga without firing a shot.

The Americans won a great victory at the Battle of Bennington.

English won this battle on July 7, 1777. But Vermont was closely linked to a major American victory. This was the Battle of Bennington. It was fought on August 16, 1777. The battle was planned in Vermont. Vermonters did much of the fighting. Yet, the battle actually took place west of Bennington in New York State.

The Americans won the war. The thirteen colonies had become the United States. Vermont was not one of the new states, though. Instead, it was a country of its own.

18

A Country Called Vermont

Vermonters made a big decision during the war. They decided not to be part of any colony, state, or country. Vermont declared its independence on January 15, 1777. Vermont was a country for the next fourteen years. At first, it was called New Connecticut.

In July 1777, a convention was held in Windsor. At that meeting, the name was changed to Vermont. Also at that meeting, Vermont officials adopted a constitution. This framework of government outlawed slavery. Vermont was the first of what are now the fifty states to ban slavery.

Thomas Chittenden was elected president of Vermont in 1778. Vermont set up relations with other countries. It even coined its own money and had a postal service.

The Fourteenth State

By 1790, many Vermonters were ready to join the United States. That year, Vermont paid New York $30,000 to settle the old land dispute. This helped pave the way for statehood. The United States Congress made Vermont the fourteenth state on

Of the fifty states, only Vermont, Texas, and California were independent countries before joining the Union.

Thomas Chittenden

Vermont was the first state added to the original thirteen.

Vermonter Justin Morgan raised and bred the first Morgan horses in the 1790s.

March 4, 1791. Thomas Chittenden became the state's first governor. Montpelier became the permanent capital in 1805.

Most Vermonters farmed in those early years. They grew corn and wheat. They used Morgan horses to plow their hilly fields. Morgan horses were named for Justin Morgan. He was the Vermonter who raised the first of them during the 1790s.

Life was difficult in the Green Mountain State. Vermonters had to overcome cold weather, rocky soil, and a lack of large towns. A weather disaster struck Vermont in 1816. Snow fell that year in June, July, and August. People starved. Crops and livestock died. The cold spell lasted two years. Many Vermonters left the state.

NEW IDEAS AND INVENTIONS

Vermonters came up with many new ideas. They also made many inventions during the early 1800s. In 1812, James Wilson of Bradford built the first American-made globe. In 1814, Emma Willard opened the country's first college-level school for women. It was in Middlebury. In 1823, Samuel Read Hall founded the country's first teacher-training school. It was in Concord.

Thaddeus Fairbanks of St. Johnsbury invented the platform scale in 1830. In 1834, Brandon blacksmith Thomas Davenport built the first electric motor. In the mid-1800s, Silas Herring built the first burglar-proof safe. He was born near Rutland. Businesses were founded to make some of these newly invented products.

Left: Inventor Thaddeus Fairbanks Right: The first American-made globe was built by James Wilson of Bradford.

THE SLAVERY ISSUE

Americans argued over slavery in the early 1800s. The southern states allowed slavery. Vermont and the other northern states had outlawed it. By the

Stephen Douglas

late 1830s, Vermont was one of the strongest anti-slavery states.

People who hated slavery helped slaves escape. They used the Underground Railroad. This was a string of hiding places that led to Canada. Once in Canada, the slaves were free. Many slaves from the South escaped through Vermont. The state still has homes with secret rooms where slaves once hid.

In 1860, Vermonters showed how much they hated slavery. Vermont-born Stephen A. Douglas ran for president that year. Abraham Lincoln ran also. Vermonters did not agree with Douglas's views on slavery. Three-fourths of them voted for Abraham Lincoln. He hadn't even visited the state.

THE CIVIL WAR

Vermont voted more heavily for Abraham Lincoln in 1860 than any other state.

Hundreds of Morgan horses also served in the Civil War.

Lincoln won the election. White southerners believed that Lincoln wanted to end slavery in the South. Eleven southern states left the Union. In April 1861, the Civil War (1861-1865) began. The southern (Confederate) states fought the northern (Union) states in this war.

Vermonters saw the Civil War as a chance to end slavery. Vermont was the first state to offer troops to the Union.

No Civil War battles were fought in Vermont. But on October 19, 1864, Confederate soldiers robbed three banks in St. Albans. Then they fled to Canada with more than $200,000 for the Confederacy. This was the northernmost action of the Civil War.

The North won the Civil War. Slavery was ended. North and South came back together as one country. More than 5,000 Vermonters had died so this could happen.

GROWTH OF DAIRYING, QUARRYING, AND INDUSTRY

After the Civil War, many Vermonters began raising dairy cows. Vermont became a milk, butter, and

During the Civil War, these Confederate soldiers helped rob three banks in northern Vermont.

cheese producer. In 1869, dairy farmers gathered in Montpelier. They formed the country's first statewide dairy association. Also in 1869, silos began to appear on Vermont farms. They were the first ones in the country. Silos store food for farm animals. Today, they can be seen on farms across America.

Quarrying and mining also gained importance. Barre became the "Granite Center of the World." Proctor became a great marble-quarrying area. Ely had copper mines.

Vermont's industries were also growing. Burlington made and shipped lumber. Organs became a major Brattleboro product. Factories in

Springfield and Bellows Falls made tools. Clothing, maple syrup, and guns also came from Vermont.

People from many lands came to work in Vermont's quarries and factories. Some came from nearby Canada. Others arrived from England, Scotland, Ireland, and Wales. Still others traveled from Italy, Greece, Poland, and Spain.

VERMONT IN THE SPOTLIGHT

In 1880, Vermont-born Chester Arthur was elected vice-president for President James Garfield. Garfield was shot only a few months after he became president. When he died in September 1881, Arthur became president. He served until 1885.

In 1898, the United States and Spain fought the Spanish-American War. Vermonter George Dewey was a naval hero of the war. Ships under Dewey destroyed Spain's fleet in the Philippines. The United States won the war. The United States also won land from Spain: the Philippines, Puerto Rico, and Guam.

The Vermont Bureau of Publicity opened in 1911. It was the first state tourist agency in the country. The bureau helped bring vacationers to Vermont. Hotels, resorts, and summer homes went

Vermont was the first state in the country to open a tourist agency.

In 1927, the first women hiked the famous Long Trail in Vermont.

up in the state. Many children from crowded cities went to summer camp in Vermont.

In 1910, the Green Mountain Club was formed. Its members decided to mark a safe trail through the Green Mountains. They marked the 262-mile Long Trail. This famous hiking trail was finished in 1928.

WORLD WARS, FLOODS, AND DEPRESSION

The United States entered World War I (1914-1918) in 1917. Vermonters again were among the first to go to war. Nearly 20,000 Vermont men and women served in the war. About 650 of them died.

In 1923, a second Vermonter became president. This was Calvin Coolidge. In 1920, he was elected vice-president. On August 3, 1923, Coolidge was at his father's Plymouth Notch home. News came that President Warren Harding had died. In the middle of the night, Coolidge's father gave him the presidential oath. In 1924, Coolidge was elected president.

Two disasters struck Vermont during the 1920s. The first was the November 1927 flood. Heavy rains caused many rivers to flood. Whole neighborhoods were washed away in some towns. About sixty people died.

The second disaster involved the whole country. In 1929, the Great Depression hit America. This period of hardship lasted ten years. Factories and farms went out of business. The United States government began programs to put people to work. These programs also helped the states through the tough times. Programs in Vermont built flood-control dams and ski trails.

The Great Depression ended in 1939. World War II (1939-1945) began that year. The United States entered the war in December 1941. Vermont had not waited until December. The state made headlines in September 1941 by declaring war on its

This boat is floating down the main street of Montpelier during the 1927 flood.

About 1,500 Vermonters died in World War II.

own. About 50,000 Vermont men and women served in World War II.

GROWTH AND THE ENVIRONMENT

Vermont's population grew slowly in the early 1900s. From 1900 to 1950, it rose from 343,641 to only 377,747 people. Many states enjoyed greater growth than that in one year!

Since 1960, though, Vermont has grown by 6,000 people a year. Many people moved to Vermont to work in tourism and industry. Skiing became very popular in Vermont during the 1970s and 1980s. New resorts opened. During those years, many companies set up business in the state.

The boom in people and industry has helped Vermont. Yet, more people and factories often mean more pollution. Pollution hurts the environment.

In 1970, Vermont passed a major law to preserve its beauty. This is the Environmental Control Law. It allows the state to control building. Developers' plans must not harm the air, water, or soil. This is a strict law. It has been a model for similar laws in other states.

Lately, Vermonters have argued over their antipollution laws. Some Vermonters say the laws

are too strict. They say that these laws cost jobs and money. Other Vermonters want strict laws. Only strict laws can keep their state green and lovely.

The popularity of skiing has helped Vermont's tourism business.

In 1984, Madeleine Kunin was elected Vermont's first woman governor. She worked to protect the environment. She also brought more women into Vermont's government. By 1992, one-third of Vermont's lawmakers were women. This was the highest percentage of women lawmakers in the fifty states. Many of them have helped pass laws to protect Vermont's environment.

Vermonters have been inventive in the past. Perhaps they will show the country how to have both beauty and growth. This is one of Vermont's great challenges as it enters the twenty-first century.

Overleaf: A lamb at the Palfrey farm in Clarendon

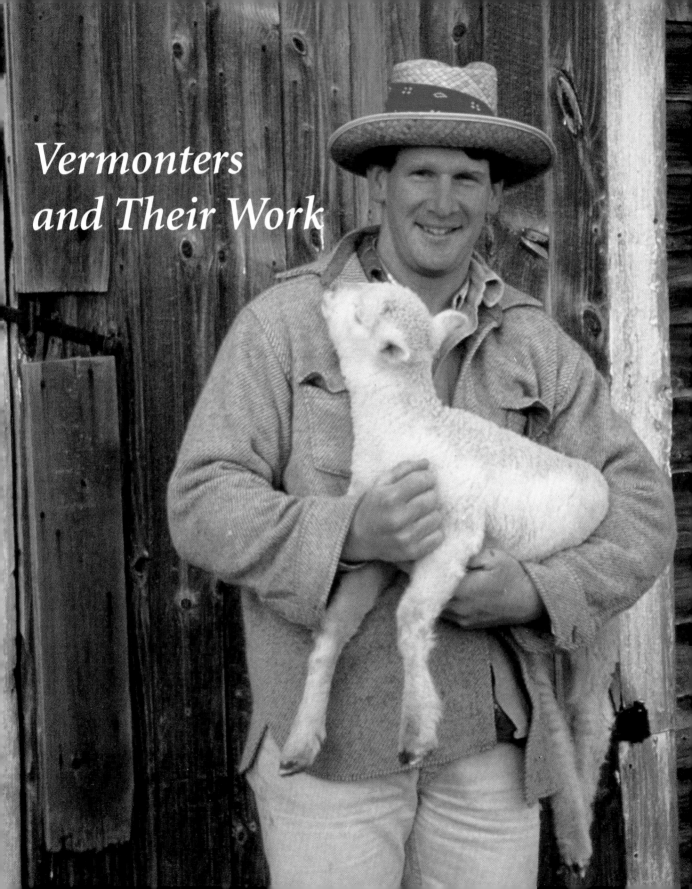

Vermonters
and Their Work

Vermonters and Their Work

The 1990 Census counted 562,758 Vermonters. Wyoming and Alaska are the only states with fewer people. Twenty United States cities have more people than Vermont.

Vermont is the most rural state. Two-thirds of Vermonters live on farms or in small towns. One-third of Vermonters live in cities. Vermont's largest city is Burlington. It has only 39,127 people. Montpelier is the capital. It has only 8,247 people. No other state has a smaller largest city or capital.

To most Vermonters, "small is beautiful." People have plenty of room in Vermont. As one girl wrote, "I like Vermont because the trees are close together and the people are far apart." Because the towns are small, Vermonters get to know their neighbors.

Nearly 99 of every 100 Vermonters are white. Vermont has few American Indians, blacks, Asians, or Hispanics. Most Vermonters are Roman Catholics or Protestants. Yet, the state offers surprises in regard to minorities.

In 1836, Vermonters elected Alexander Twilight to the state legislature. Twilight became

Wyoming has the fewest people of any state. About 454,000 people live in Wyoming.

Two-thirds of Vermonters live on farms or in small towns.

America's first black state lawmaker. In 1990, Madeleine Kunin was elected for the fourth time as governor. She is Jewish. How did these things happen in a state with so few black people or Jewish people?

Vermonters tend to see people as individuals. Perhaps they can do this because there are so few Vermonters. How people do their jobs means more than their sex, religion, or color.

TOWN MEETINGS AND STATE GOVERNMENT

Vermonters have a strong voice in their government. On the first Tuesday each March, the people gather for town meetings. People take a direct part in government at town meetings. They elect the town's officials. They also pass laws.

A governor heads each state's government in the United States. In forty-seven states, the governors serve four-year terms. Only in Vermont, New Hampshire, and Rhode Island do they serve two-year terms. Those voters feel that short terms keep governors on their toes. Vermont's lawmakers in the house and senate also have two-year terms.

Town meetings have been held in New England since the 1600s.

THEIR WORK

More than 270,000 Vermonters have jobs. About 80,000 of them do service work. Many of these people serve tourists. They work at ski resorts and

Outdoor sports are popular year-round activities in Vermont.

hotels. Other service workers include nurses, doctors, and car mechanics. Banking and insurance provide other service jobs.

About 50,000 Vermonters make products. Computer parts and electrical equipment are the state's leading goods. Other products include packaged foods, tools, paper, books, guns, and tombstones. Another 62,000 Vermonters sell goods.

Vermont has more than 40,000 government workers. Many of them are teachers. The building industry is also important in Vermont.

About 11,000 people work on Vermont's 7,000 farms. Milk is the state's leading farm product.

Other farm goods include potatoes, apples, eggs, honey, and beef cattle. Vermont leads the country at making maple syrup. Maple sugar, candies, and soft drinks are made from maple syrup.

About 500 Vermonters work in quarries. Vermont is a big producer of granite and marble. Many of the country's public buildings contain granite and marble from Vermont. Vermont marble went into the United States Capitol and the Supreme Court Building. Limestone, slate, and sand and gravel are other Vermont quarry products.

Overleaf: A house and covered bridge in Green River

Left: A Vermont granite quarry Right: Collecting sap from a sugar maple tree is the first step in making maple syrup.

A Trip Through the Green Mountain State

A Trip Through the Green Mountain State

V ermont is a wonderful place to visit. The state has lovely mountains, valleys, lakes, and woods. Visitors enjoy skiing, snowmobiling, swimming, canoeing, hiking, and biking. Vermont's cities and small towns also attract visitors.

The Bennington Battle Monument honors the Americans who won the Battle of Bennington.

Southern Vermont

Bennington is a good place to start a tour of the state. It is near Vermont's southwest corner. Bennington was founded in 1750. Today, it is Vermont's third-largest city. Bennington College is located there.

Bennington's Catamount Tavern is gone. A statue of a catamount guards the spot today. Nearby is the Bennington Battle Monument. It is 306 feet tall. It was built to honor the Americans who won the Battle of Bennington.

The United States adopted the Stars and Stripes as its flag in June 1777. A similar flag was flown two months later at the Battle of Bennington. That flag is now the oldest known Stars and Stripes. It can be seen at the Bennington Museum.

Brattleboro is directly east across the state from *Brattleboro*
Bennington. This isn't a long trip. Vermont is only
45 miles wide at this point. Each February,
Brattleboro has ski-jumping contests. The
Brattleboro Museum and Art Center is in an old
train station. Old Estey organs can be seen there.
Brattleboro's Estey Organ Company was one of
America's largest organ makers. Today, this city on
the Connecticut River is Vermont's sixth-largest
city.

North from Brattleboro is Bellows Falls. It is
also on the Connecticut River. The Green
Mountain Flyer runs out of Bellows Falls. It is a

Above: The one-room Eureka Schoolhouse in Springfield
Below left: The Windsor covered bridge
Below right: The Calvin Coolidge Birthplace and Homestead in Plymouth Notch

sightseeing train. River valleys and waterfalls can be seen on its 26-mile trip.

Springfield is north of Bellows Falls. Vermont's oldest school that is still standing is located there. This is the one-room Eureka Schoolhouse. It was built in 1790.

Windsor is a short way north of Springfield. It is called the "Birthplace of Vermont." The Old Constitution House is in Windsor. Vermont's first constitution was adopted there in 1777.

The country's longest covered bridge can be seen at Windsor. This bridge is 450 feet long. It crosses the Connecticut River to Cornish, New Hampshire. Vermont has more than 100 covered bridges. That is more than any other state has.

CENTRAL VERMONT

Northwest of Windsor is Plymouth Notch. Calvin Coolidge Birthplace and Homestead is there. Visitors can see the bed where Coolidge was born. The room where Coolidge took the oath to become president can also be seen.

Rutland is northwest of Coolidge's birthplace. Rutland was settled in 1770. With 18,230 people, Rutland is Vermont's second-largest city. The Norman Rockwell Museum is a highlight of the Rutland area. Rockwell was a famous artist. He did scenes of typical American life. He lived in Vermont for fourteen years. Vermonters served as models for many Rockwell pictures. The museum displays his work.

Proctor is north of Rutland. It is a center for processing marble. The Vermont Marble Exhibit in Proctor tells how marble is formed. Artists show how marble is finished and carved. The museum has a big collection of Vermont marble.

Middlebury is northwest of Rutland. Middlebury College, founded in 1800, is Vermont's oldest private college. The Emma Willard House is on the Middlebury College campus. Here, Willard founded her famous school for women.

This sculptor at the Vermont Marble Company in Proctor is working with a piece of Rutland marble.

41

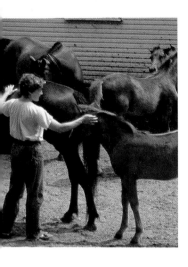

The University of Vermont runs the Morgan Horse Farm.

Montpelier was named for Montpellier, a city in France. The name means "bare hill" in French.

The Morgan Horse Farm is near Middlebury at Weybridge. Morgan horses are bred there. People around the country buy these horses. They use them for trail riding, showing, and farm work.

Barre is near Vermont's exact center. It is still called the "Granite Center of the World." The Rock of Ages Quarry is near Barre. It is one of the world's largest granite quarries. Visitors can watch 200,000-pound granite blocks being lifted from the quarry. The country's first Boy Scout troop was organized in Barre in 1909. Today, Barre is Vermont's fifth-largest city.

Montpelier is northwest of Barre. Settled around 1787, Montpelier has been Vermont's capital since 1805. Vermont lawmakers meet in the state capitol in Montpelier. Vermonters call this beautiful building their State House. It is made of Vermont granite.

The Vermont Historical Society Museum is near the State House. It has exhibits on Vermont history. The stuffed catamount is a favorite among visitors. It dates from 1881 and was the last catamount shot in Vermont.

A famous ski-resort town is a few miles north of Montpelier. This is Stowe, where many great champions have skied.

NORTHERN VERMONT

Northeastern Vermont has very few people. There are fewer people here than in any other part of the state. Vermonters call this region the Northeast Kingdom. It is a land of lovely woods, lakes, and farms.

St. Johnsbury is the Northeast Kingdom's largest city. It has just over 6,000 people. St. Johnsbury is a maple syrup-producing area. At Maple Grove Farms, visitors can see how maple syrup is made. The Fairbanks Museum and Planetarium is also in St. Johnsbury. It has displays on animals, the weather, and the stars.

*Left: The state capitol in Montpelier
Right: The Rock of Ages granite quarry near Barre*

The Fairbanks Museum and Planetarium was founded by Franklin Fairbanks, nephew of platform scale inventor Thaddeus Fairbanks.

Flowers blooming at the Vermont Wildflower Farm near Charlotte

Across the state, in northwestern Vermont, is the Lake Champlain area. The Vermont Wildflower Farm is there near Charlotte. Hundreds of kinds of wildflowers grow at the farm. Each spring, they fill the farm with bright colors and sweet smells.

The Shelburne Museum is north of Charlotte near Shelburne. It is one of the best museums in all of New England. Many buildings date from the 1700s and 1800s. They were moved to Shelburne from other places in and near Vermont. The buildings include old homes, shops, and a jail. The *Ticonderoga* is also at the Shelburne Museum. It was the last steamboat to operate on Lake Champlain.

Burlington is just north of Shelburne. It was settled in 1773. Burlington today is Vermont's largest city. It has 39,127 people. The Green

Mountains are east of the city. Lake Champlain is to the west. Burlington is called the "Queen City of Vermont" because of its lovely location. From there, many people take cruises on Lake Champlain.

Ethan Allen lived in Burlington. His farmhouse was built around 1785. It is open to visitors. The University of Vermont is also in Burlington. It is the state's largest school of higher education.

Several islands in Lake Champlain belong to Vermont. North and South Hero Islands and Isle La Motte are the largest. The Hyde Log Cabin is on South Hero Island. Built in 1783, it is one of the country's oldest log cabins. The French built Fort St. Anne on Isle La Motte in 1666. St. Anne's Shrine, a little chapel, now stands there.

St. Albans is a good place to end this trip. It is near Vermont's northwestern corner. Escaped slaves tried to reach St. Albans. It was just 15 miles from Canada and freedom. St. Albans has buildings where escaped slaves were hidden. The Franklin County Museum has displays on the famous Confederate raid on the town. Now, St. Albans hosts the Vermont Maple Festival each spring. Visitors enjoy "sugar-on-snow." Freshly boiled syrup is poured onto clean snow. The cold snow turns the hot syrup into soft taffy.

One of the buildings at the Shelburne Museum, which was founded by Electra Havemeyer Webb

Overleaf: President Chester Arthur

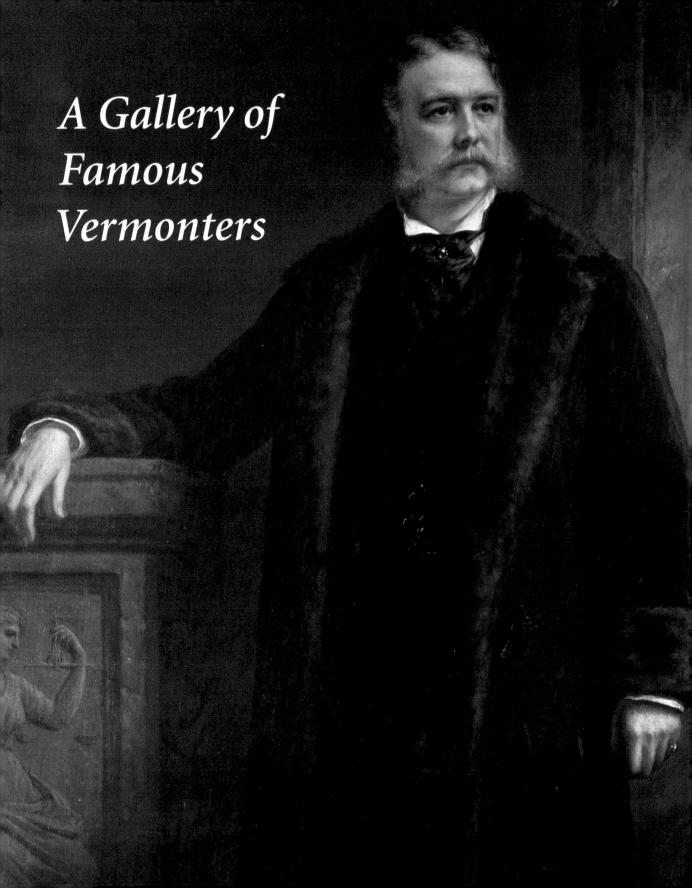

A Gallery of
Famous
Vermonters

A GALLERY OF FAMOUS VERMONTERS

Many famous people have been Vermonters. They include inventors, presidents, and even an expert on snowflakes.

Ethan Allen (1738-1789) was born in Connecticut. In 1769, he moved to the New Hampshire Grants in Vermont. He led the Green Mountain Boys against New Yorkers who wanted Vermont land. Allen was captured by the English in 1775 during the Revolutionary War. He was a prisoner for nearly three years. Allen's last years were spent on his Burlington farm.

Ira Allen (1751-1814) was also born in Connecticut but moved to Vermont. Ira served under his brother Ethan in the Green Mountain Boys. Ira Allen helped write Vermont's first constitution in 1777. He also founded the University of Vermont. Vermont became a state partly because of his work.

Alexander Twilight (1795-1857) was born in Corinth. Twilight was the country's first black college graduate and state legislator. He graduated from Middlebury College in 1823. He founded

Ethan Allen

Alexander Twilight

Brownington Academy in the 1830s. Twilight was elected to the Vermont legislature in 1836.

Zerah Colburn (1804-1839) was born in Cabot. As a young boy, he could quickly do hard math problems in his head. Colburn traveled around the United States and Europe. He put on shows as a human computer. He answered such questions as how many seconds had passed since the birth of Christ.

Historian **Abby Hemenway** (1828-1890) was born in Ludlow. She spoke to many people about the history of Vermont's towns. Hemenway wrote a 6,000-page history of Vermont.

Larkin Mead (1835-1910) was born in New Hampshire. He grew up in Brattleboro. When he was twenty-one, Mead made a snow sculpture. Not many people did snow sculptures at that time. Later, Mead designed the statues at Abraham Lincoln's tomb in Springfield, Illinois. The Ethan Allen statue in the U.S. Capitol is also his work.

Wilson A. " Snowflake" Bentley (1865-1931) was born in Jericho. Bentley built a career out of snow. He designed a camera with a microscope lens. With it, Bentley took thousands of pictures of snowflakes. By studying the pictures, he discovered that no two snowflakes are alike.

Larkin Mead

Elisha Otis (1811-1861) was born in the Vermont town of Halifax. In 1853, he invented the first modern elevator. Today, Otis elevators are in buildings around the world.

Two Vermonters established a new religion during the 1800s. **Joseph Smith** (1805-1844) was born in Sharon. In 1830, he founded the Mormon Church in New York State. Smith was murdered in Illinois. **Brigham Young** (1801-1877), who was born in Whitingham, then became the Mormon leader. Young led the Mormons to Utah. Many Mormons live there today. Young served as the Utah Territory's first governor (1849-1857).

The Mormon Church is officially called the Church of Jesus Christ of Latter-day Saints.

Brigham Young (left) meeting Mormon leader Joseph Smith (right) for the first time

President Calvin Coolidge throwing out the first pitch at a baseball game

Justin Smith Morrill

George Perkins Marsh (1801-1882) was born in Woodstock. He was concerned about saving the environment. Marsh wrote a book on the subject in 1864. It was called *Man and Nature.*

Justin Smith Morrill (1810-1898) was born in Strafford. At the age of fifteen, he stopped going to school. He had to get a job. Later, Morrill served for forty-four years in the U.S. House (1855-1867) and Senate (1867-1899). Morrill remembered how he had missed out on college. He helped pass the

Morrill Land-Grant College Act of 1862. This law set up many state universities.

Chester Alan Arthur (1829-1886) was probably born in Fairfield. He taught at North Pownal Academy (1848-1853). Later, he became a lawyer in New York. In 1881, he became the twenty-first president when President James Garfield died.

Calvin Coolidge (1872-1933) was born in Plymouth Notch. He, too, became a lawyer. Coolidge was vice-president (1921-1923) for President Warren Harding. When Harding died, Coolidge became the thirtieth president (1923-1929). Coolidge let his pet raccoon, Rebecca, run around the White House. Coolidge also had a kitten named Tige. He often walked through the White House with Tige draped around his neck.

Dorothy Canfield Fisher

Dorothy Canfield Fisher (1879-1958) was born in Kansas. She moved to Arlington, Vermont, about 1907. Fisher became a famous author. She wrote *Understood Betsy*, a popular children's book.

Katherine Paterson was born in China in 1932. Later, she settled in Vermont. Paterson also is a children's book author. She has won two Newbery Medals. Paterson won the 1978 Newbery for *Bridge to Terabithia*. She won again in 1981 for *Jacob Have I Loved*.

Skier Andrea Mead Lawrence (above left), baseball star Carlton Fisk (above right), and singer Rudy Vallee (below) were born in Vermont.

Rudy Vallee (1901-1986) was born in Island Pond. He became a famous singer. Many older people remember hearing him sing "My Time Is Your Time" on the radio. Vallee also made many movies.

Several great athletes have been Vermonters. **Andrea Mead Lawrence** was born in Rutland in 1932. She began skiing when she was three. In 1952, Lawrence won two Olympic gold medals in skiing. She became the first U.S. woman to do that. Baseball star **Carlton Fisk** was born in 1947 in Bellows Falls. He became one of the greatest catchers in big-league history. In 1990, he hit his 328th home run. That was an all-time record for a catcher.

Madeleine Kunin was born in Switzerland in 1933. She came to the United States in 1940. She

GOVERNOR
KUNIN
Vermont

worked as a reporter for the *Burlington Free Press* for a time. Kunin served in the Vermont house of representatives (1973-1979) and as lieutenant governor (1979-1983). Later, she was Vermont's governor (1985-1991). In 1993, she was appointed Deputy Secretary of the U.S. Department of Education.

Madeleine Kunin

Home to Madeleine Kunin, Ethan Allen, Abby Hemenway, and "Snowflake" Bentley . . .

Producer of granite, marble, maple syrup, milk, and computers . . .

The state that first outlawed slavery, and where America's first Boy Scout troop began . . .

A land of green mountains and blue lakes . . .

This is Vermont, the Green Mountain State!

Did You Know?

Vermont has towns and villages named Beanville, Bread Loaf, Goose Green, Maple Corner, Orange, and Tinmouth.

Queenie, a water-skiing elephant who appeared on television shows, lived on an animal farm in Fairlee.

Jewelry and wallpaper patterns have been designed after Wilson Bentley's photos of snowflakes. His pictures also inspire the snowflakes that children cut out.

Ben and Jerry's Ice Cream has its headquarters in Waterbury.

The National Rotten Sneaker Championship is held on the first day of spring in Montpelier. The prizes are savings bonds, new sneakers, and foot powder.

In 1954, Consuelo N. Bailey was elected the first woman lieutenant governor of a state.

A woman once told Calvin Coolidge: "I have made a bet that I could get more than two words out of you." "Silent Cal" answered: "You lose!"

Burlington doctor H. Nelson Jackson was the first person to cross the country by car. In 1903, Dr. Jackson took seventy days to cross the United States in a car called the *Vermont*.

The "251 Club" is famous in Vermont. Its members try to visit all 251 of Vermont's towns and cities. About 225 of the club's 3,000 members have done this.

One kind of coin made in Vermont in 1785 is worth as much as $3,000 today.

In the mid-1800s, Joel Ellis of Springfield made the country's first doll carriages. Ellis also made the country's first dolls with movable body parts.

Zerah Colburn was once asked how many seconds there are in 2,000 years. The boy correctly answered: "Sixty-three billion and seventy-two million seconds."

Vermont's first governor, Thomas Chittenden, called Vermont "the home of freedom and unity." "Freedom and Unity" became the state motto.

Rope tows pull skiers up hills. The first rope tow in the United States was used in Woodstock, Vermont, in 1934. It was powered by a Model T Ford engine.

Deane Davis was a member of the first Boy Scout troop in the United States. It met in Barre in 1909. Sixty years later Davis became governor of Vermont.

VERMONT INFORMATION

State flag

Honeybees

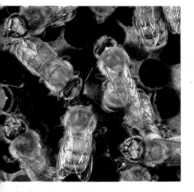

Monarch butterfly

Area: 9,614 square miles (only seven states are smaller)

Greatest Distance North to South: 158 miles

Greatest Distance East to West: 97 miles

Borders: Canada to the north; New Hampshire to the east; Massachusetts to the south; New York to the west

Highest Point: Mount Mansfield, 4,393 feet above sea level

Lowest Point: Lake Champlain, 95 feet above sea level

Hottest Recorded Temperature: 105° F. (at Vernon, on July 4, 1911)

Coldest Recorded Temperature: -50° F. (at Bloomfield, on December 30, 1933)

Statehood: The fourteenth state, on March 4, 1791

Origin of Name: Vermont is from the French words *vert* and *mont*, which mean "green mountain"

Capital: Montpelier since 1805

Counties: 14

United States Senators: 2

United States Representatives: 1 (as of 1992)

State Senators: 30

State Representatives: 150

State Song: "Hail, Vermont!" by Josephine Hovey Perry

State Motto: "Freedom and Unity" (coined by Thomas Chittenden)

Nickname: "Green Mountain State"

State Seal: Adopted in 1779

State Flag: Adopted in 1923

State Flower: Red clover

State Bird: Hermit thrush

State Tree: Sugar maple

State Animal: Morgan horse

State Insect: Honeybee

State Butterfly: Monarch butterfly

State Fish: Brook trout and walleye pike

State Beverage: Milk

Main Mountain Ranges: Green Mountains, Taconic Mountains

Some Rivers: Otter Creek, Winooski, Lamoille, Missisquoi, Connecticut, White, Black, West, Mad, Ottauquechee

Some Lakes: Champlain, Memphremagog, Bomoseen, Willoughby, Carmi, St. Catherine, Seymour

Wildlife: Deer, foxes, beavers, minks, bears, skunks, rabbits, squirrels, raccoons, porcupines, woodchucks, bobcats, otters, moose, muskrats, thrushes, cardinals, geese, wild turkeys, many other kinds of birds, trout, walleye pike, many other kinds of fish

Farm Products: Milk, potatoes, apples, eggs, honey, beef cattle, maple syrup, Christmas trees, Morgan horses, sheep, oats, corn

Manufactured Products: Computer parts, electrical equipment, tools and other metal goods, ice cream, cheese, other packaged foods, books, paper, canoes, tombstones

Mining Products: Granite, marble, slate, sand and gravel, limestone

Population: 562,758, forty-eighth among the fifty states (1990 U.S. Census Bureau figures)

Major Cities (1990 Census):

Burlington	39,127	Hartford	9,404
Rutland	18,230	Brattleboro	8,612
South Burlington	12,809	Essex Junction	8,396
Bennington	9,532	Montpelier	8,247
Barre	9,482	St. Albans	7,339

Hermit thrush

Brook trout

Red fox

VERMONT HISTORY

The Champlain Monument on Isle La Motte

10,000 B.C.—Prehistoric Indians reach Vermont

A.D. 1300-1750—American Indians inhabit the Vermont area

1609—Samuel de Champlain becomes the first known explorer in Vermont and claims the region for France

1666—The French build Fort St. Anne on Isle La Motte

1690—The English build a fort near what is now Addison

1724—England's Massachusetts colony builds Fort Dummer, Vermont's first permanent European settlement

1749—New Hampshire governor Benning Wentworth begins granting land in Vermont, called the New Hampshire Grants

1763—England gains clear control over Vermont

1764—The king of England rules that Vermont belongs to New York

1770—The Green Mountain Boys fight New York's claim

1775—The Green Mountain Boys capture Fort Ticonderoga

1777—Vermont declares itself a country on January 15; on July 7, the English win the Battle of Hubbardton; on August 16, the Americans win the Battle of Bennington

1783—The peace treaty that ends the Revolutionary War is signed

1790—Vermont pays New York $30,000 to settle the land dispute

1791—On March 4, Vermont becomes the fourteenth state

1805—Montpelier becomes the permanent state capital

1816—The "year without a summer" occurs, with frost or snow in every summer month

1850—Vermont's population reaches 314,120

1861—As the Civil War starts, Vermont is the first state to offer troops to the Union

1864—Confederates raid banks in St. Albans

1865—The Civil War ends; more than 5,000 of the 35,000 Vermonters who served have died

1869—Vermont is the site of the country's first state dairy association and its earliest silos

1881—Chester Arthur becomes the twenty-first president of the United States

1898—Vermonter George Dewey is a naval hero of the Spanish-American War

1909—The country's first Boy Scout troop is organized in Barre

1910—Work on the Long Trail is begun

1917-18—Nearly 20,000 Vermonters help win World War I; about 650 of them die

1923—Calvin Coolidge becomes the thirtieth president of the United States

1927—Nearly sixty people die in the November floods

1928—The Long Trail is finished

1929-39—During the Great Depression, many Vermonters lose their farms and jobs; the government puts people to work building flood-control dams and ski trails

1941—In September, Vermont declares its entry into World War II; in December, the United States enters the war

1945—World War II ends; about 1,500 of the 50,000 Vermont men and women who served have died

1970—The Environmental Control Law is passed

1984—Madeleine Kunin is elected as Vermont's first woman governor

1991—Happy 200th birthday, Green Mountain State!

1992—Spring floods hit Montpelier and several other Vermont towns

1994—Governor Howard Dean is reelected to a second term

George Dewey

MAP KEY

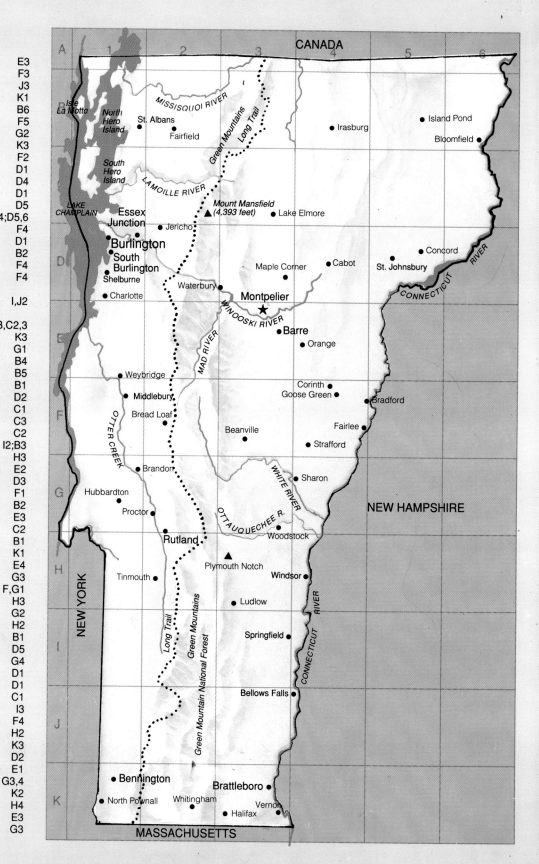

GLOSSARY

ancient: Relating to a time early in history

antipollution: Laws meant to keep the environment clean

antislavery: Against slavery

billion: A thousand million (1,000,000,000)

capital: The city that is the seat of government

capitol: The building in which the government meets

catamount: A name used in the past for a mountain lion

climate: The typical weather of a region

colony: A settlement that is outside a parent country and that is ruled by the parent country

constitution: A framework for government

environment: The air, water, soil and other surroundings

explorer: A person who visits and studies unknown lands

glacier: A slowly moving sheet of ice

independence: Freedom from being controlled by another

industry: A kind of business that has many workers to make products

legislature: The lawmaking body of a state or country

million: A thousand thousand (1,000,000)

monument: A building or statue that honors a person or a famous event

Morgan horses: A kind of horse bred in Vermont and used for riding or farm work; named for Justin Morgan

patent: Papers that grant people rights to their inventions

planetarium: A machine that projects images of heavenly bodies on a ceiling; the room or building in which such a machine is used

pollution: The harming of the environment

population: The number of people in a place

prehistoric: Belonging to the time before written history

quarry: A large pit from which rock such as granite or marble is removed

rural: Relating to small towns and farm areas rather than big cities

sculpture: Statues and other three-dimensional artworks

slavery: A practice in which some people are owned by other people

tourism: The business of providing services such as food and lodging for travelers

town meeting: A meeting in which the people of a town choose their officials and decide other local matters

Underground Railroad: A series of places where slaves hid while escaping to Canada

PICTURE ACKNOWLEDGMENTS

Front cover, © Fred M. Dole/**New England Stock Photo**; 1, © Fred M. Dole/**New England Stock Photo**; 2, **Tom Dunnington**; 3, © Art Paneuf/**New England Stock Photo**; 5, **Tom Dunnington**; 6-7, © **Gene Ahrens**; 8 (left), **courtesy of Hammond, Incorporated, Maplewood, New Jersey**; 8 (right), © W. H. Clark/**H. Armstrong Roberts**; 9 (top), © Fred M. Dole/**New England Stock Photo**; 9 (bottom), © Alden Pellett/**Tony Stone Worldwide/Chicago, Ltd.**; 10, © **Gene Ahrens**; 11 (left), © Fred M. Dole/**New England Stock Photo**; 11 (right), © F. Sieb/**H. Armstrong Roberts**; 12 (detail), **Shelburne Museum, Shelburne, Vermont**, photograph by Ken Burris; 13, © W.H. Clark/**H. Armstrong Roberts**; 14, © Lawrence F. Willard/**New England Stock Photo**; 15, **Historical Pictures/Stock Montage**; 16, **The Bettmann Archive**; 17, **Historical Pictures/Stock Montage**; 18, **Historical Pictures/Stock Montage**; 19, **Vermont Historical Society**; 20, © Richard L. Capps/**R/C Photo Agency**; 21 (both pictures), **Vermont Historical Society**; 22, **Library of Congress**; 23, **Special Collections, University of Vermont Library**; 24, © James Blank/**Root Resources**; 25, **Vermont Historical Society**; 26, **Vermont Historical Society**; 27, **AP/Wide World Photos**; 29, © Brooks Dodge/**New England Stock Photo**; 30, © Margo Taussig Pinkerton/**New England Stock Photo**; 31, © **Joseph A. DiChello, Jr.**; 32, © **Joseph A. DiChello, Jr.**; 33 (both pictures), © **SuperStock, Inc.**; 34 (top), © **Joseph A. DiChello, Jr.**; 34 (bottom), © Kenneth Martin/**Armstock**; 35 (left), © Kevin Shields/**New England Stock Photo**; 35 (right), © Paul E. Clark/**New England Stock Photo**; 36-37, © Fred M. Dole/**New England Stock Photo**; 38, © H. Abernathy/**H. Armstrong Roberts**; 39, © DAMM/ZEFA/**H. Armstrong Roberts**; 40 (top), © **North Wind Pictures**; 40 (bottom left), © **Joseph A. DiChello, Jr.**; 40 (bottom right), © **SuperStock**; 41, © Michael Philip Manheim/**MGA/Photri, Inc.**; 42, © Michael Philip Manheim/**MGA/Photri, Inc.**; 43 (left), © **SuperStock**; 43 (right), © Lia Munson/**Root Resources**; 44, © **North Wind Pictures**; 45, **Vermont Travel Division, Montpelier**; 46, **White House Historical Association/photograph by the National Geographic Society**; 47 (top), © **Photri, Inc.**; 47 (bottom), **courtesy of the Orleans County Historical Society, Brownington, Vermont**; 48, **Dictionary of American Portraits**; 49, **Museum of Church History and Art, Salt Lake City, Utah**; 50 (both pictures), **Historical Pictures/Stock Montage**; 51, **AP/Wide World Photos**; 52 (top, both pictures), **AP/Wide World Photos**; 52 (bottom), **Historical Pictures/Stock Montage**; 53, **AP/Wide World Photos**; 54 (bottom), **courtesy of Elizabeth Green Dane**; 54-55 (top), **Vermont Historical Society**; 55 (bottom), **courtesy of the American Numismatic Association**; 56 (top), **courtesy Flag Research Center, Winchester, Massachusetts 01890**; 56 (middle), © Sharon Cummings/**Dembinsky Photo Assoc.**; 56 (bottom), © VISU Photography Thomas W. Chase/**New England Stock Photo**; 57 (top), © **Jerry Hennen**; 57 (middle), © Kenneth Martin/**Amstock**; 57 (bottom), © Gary Meszaros/**Dembinsky Photo Assoc.**; 58, © E. Drifmeyer/**Photri, Inc.**; 59, **Historical Pictures/Stock Montage, Inc.**; 60, **Tom Dunnington**; back cover, © **Gene Ahrens**

INDEX

Page numbers in boldface type indicate illustrations.

ABOUT THE AUTHOR

Dennis Brindell Fradin is the author of 150 published children's books. His works for Childrens Press include the Young People's Stories of Our States series, the Disaster! series, and the Thirteen Colonies series. Dennis is married to Judith Bloom Fradin, who taught high-school and college English for many years. She is now Dennis's chief researcher. The Fradins are the parents of two sons, Anthony and Michael, and a daughter, Diana. Dennis graduated from Northwestern University in 1967 with a B.A. in creative writing, and has lived in Evanston, Illinois, since that year.